SCHIRMER'S LIBRARY
OF MUSICAL CLASSICS

Vol. 2107

Scales and Finger Exercises

Upper Elementary to Lower Intermediate

Berens, Czerny, Hanon, Plaidy, Schmitt, Wieck

Includes All Major and Minor Scales

ISBN 978-1-4950-0547-3

G. SCHIRMER, Inc.

DISTRIBUTED BY

HAL•LEONARD®
CORPORATION
7777 W. BLUEMOUND RD. P.O. BOX 13819 MILWAUKEE, WI 53213

www.musicsalesclassical.com
www.halleonard.com

CONTENTS

TRAINING OF THE LEFT HAND
Op. 89, Book 1

Edited by
Theodore Baker

Hermann Berens
(1826–1880)

It is the aim of these exercises to impart velocity, strength and evenness of touch to the fingers. Any one having the patience to take up six or eight numbers daily and practise them from ten to fifteen minutes, will soon be convinced of their usefulness. Begin in a moderate tempo, increasing it at each repetition.

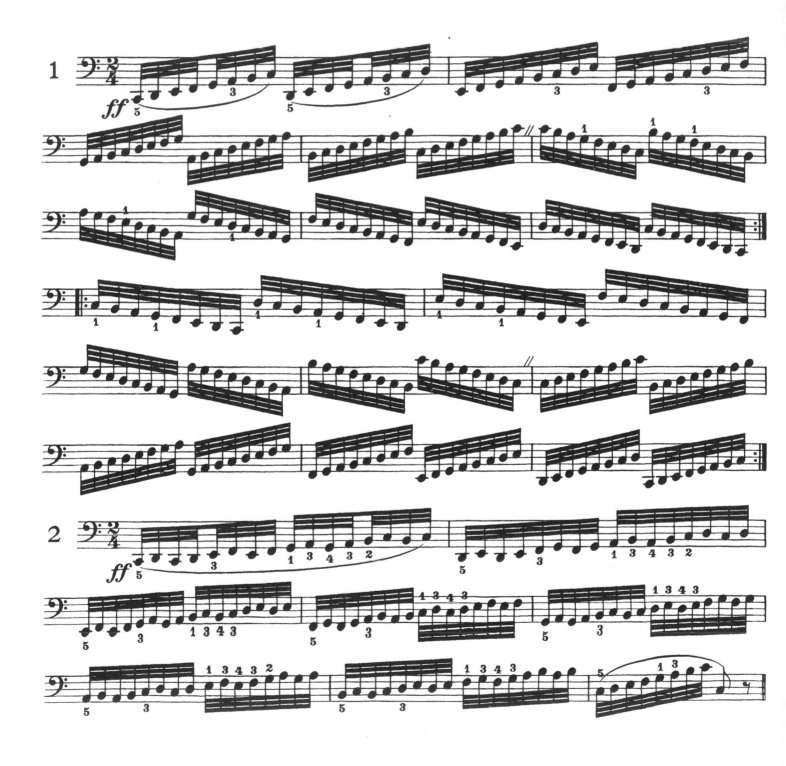

Where two fingerings are given, they should be practised alternately.

PRACTICAL FINGER EXERCISES
Op. 802, Book 1

Edited by
Max Rolle

Carl Czerny
(1791–1857)

Section I
Exercises for the five fingers, with quiet hand and fingers equally bent.

Throughout this work, each division enclosed between the signs of repetition must be played through at least ten times, one after another, without interruption, so as to form one continuous exercise. The tempo is to be taken somewhat quicker daily, according to increasing skill, in order to attain the highest possible degree of velocity compatible with clearness and accuracy.

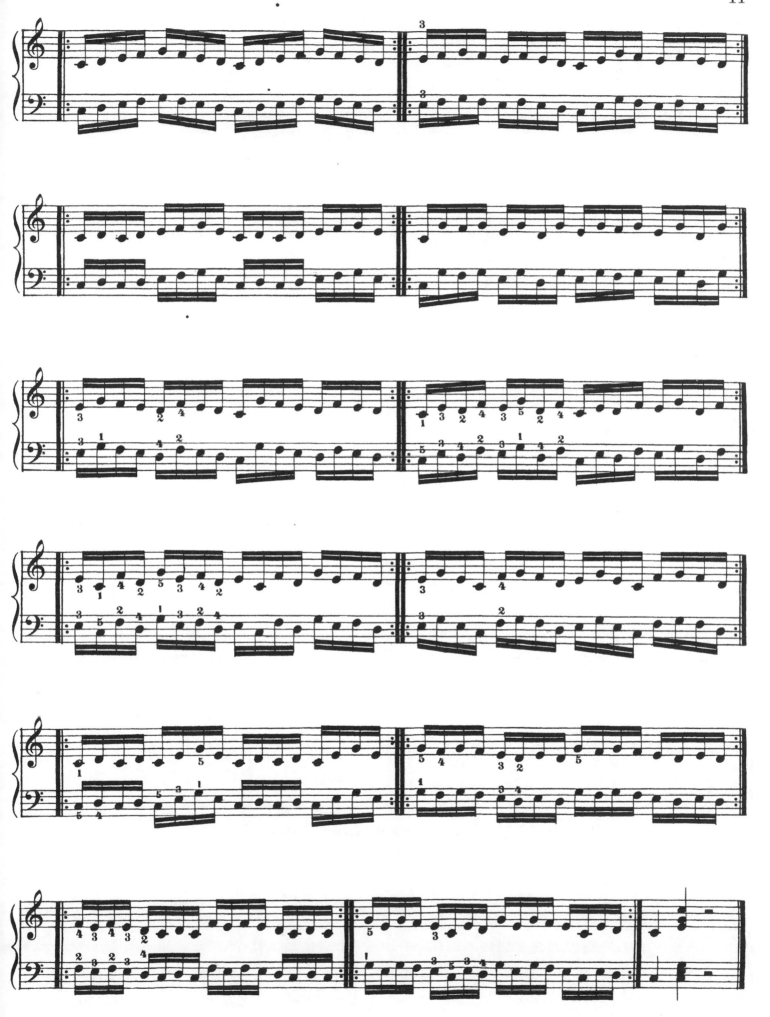

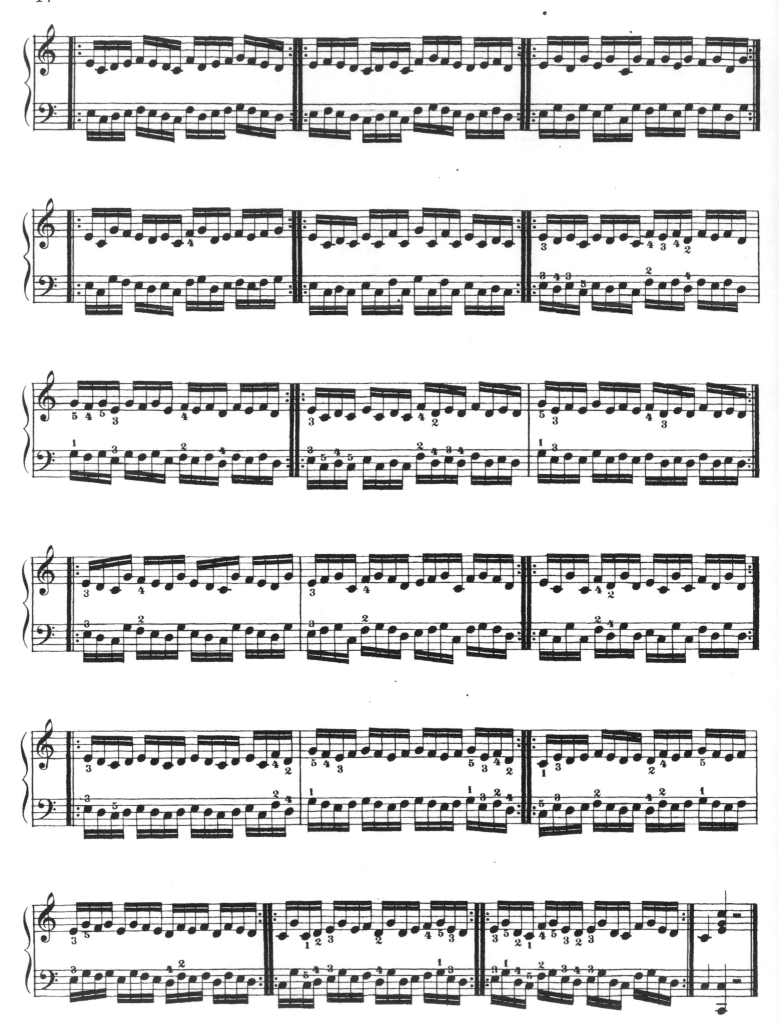

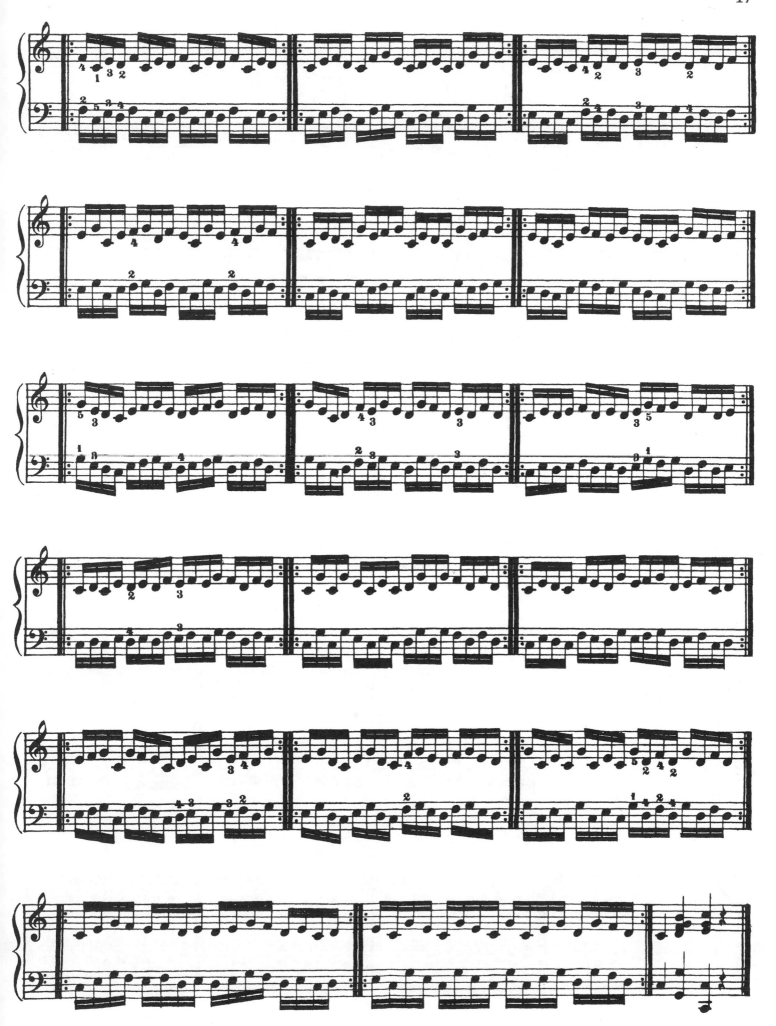

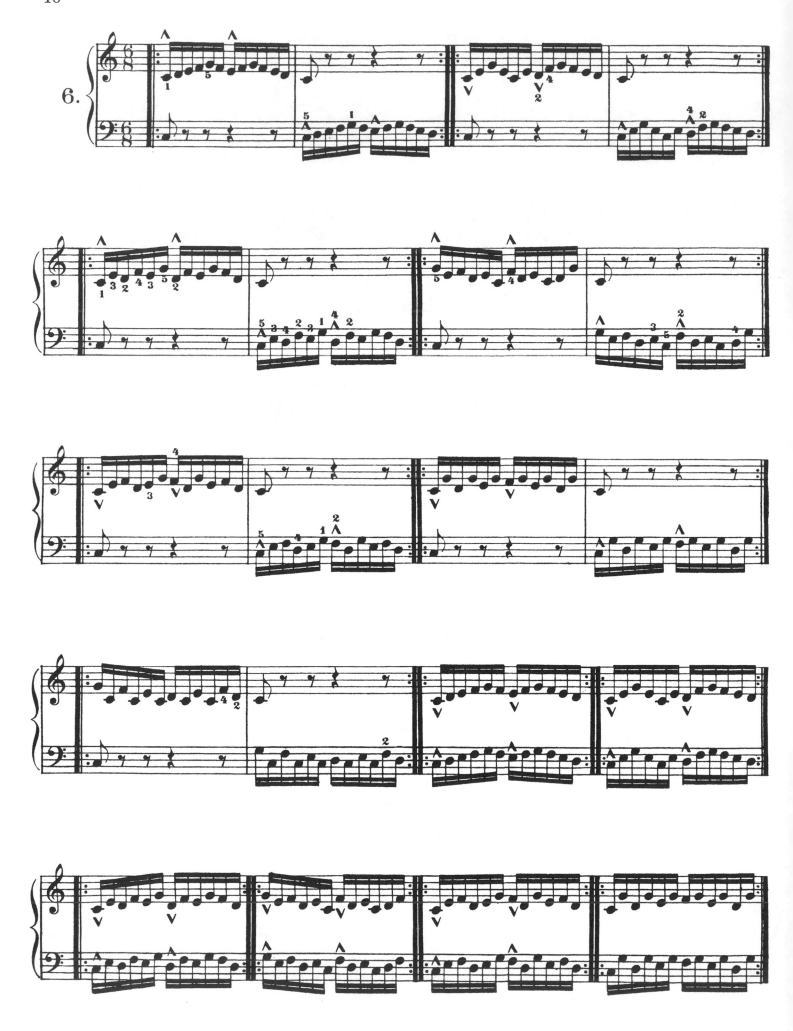

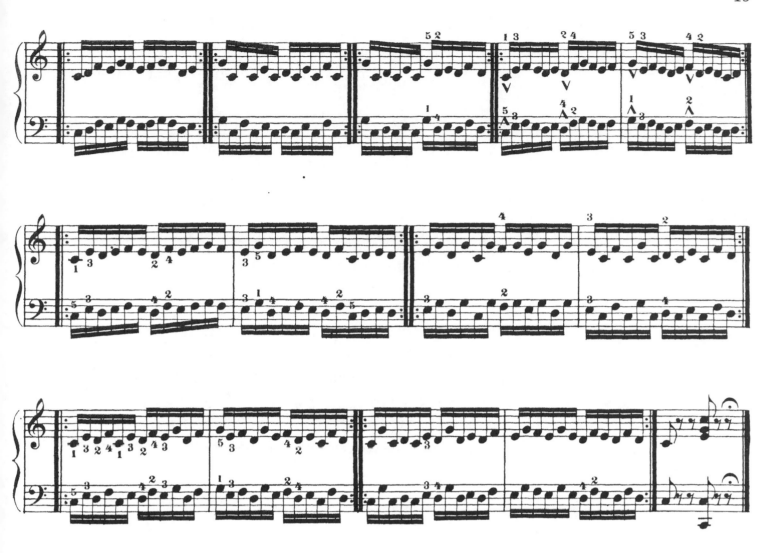

THE VIRTUOSO·PIANIST

Book 1, Part 1

Charles-Louis Hanon
(1819–1900)

Preparatory Exercises for the Acquirement of Agility, Independence, Strength and Perfect Evenness in the Fingers.

Stretch between the fifth and fourth fingers of the left hand in ascending, and the fifth and fourth fingers of the right hand in descending.

For studying the **20** exercises in this First Part, begin with the metronome set at **60**, gradually increasing the speed up to **108**; this is the meaning of the double metronome-mark at the head of each exercise.

Lift the fingers high and with precision, playing each note very distinctly.

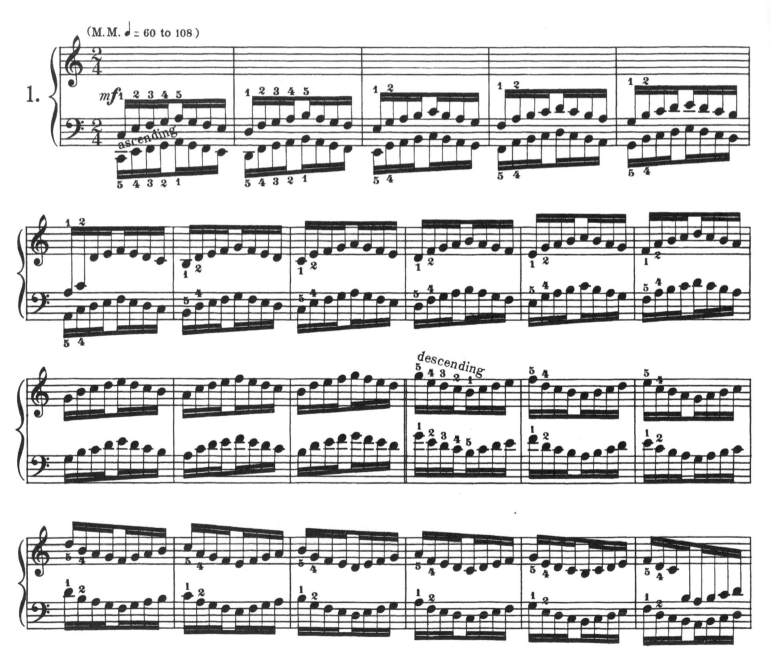

(1) For brevity, we shall henceforward indicate only by their figures those fingers which are to be specially trained in each exercise; e.g., 3–4 in № 2; 2–3–4 in № 3, etc.

Observe that, throughout the book, both hands are continually executing the same difficulties; in this way the left hand becomes as skilful as the right. Besides, the difficulties executed by the left hand in ascending, are exactly copied by the same fingers of the right hand in descending; this new style of exercise will cause the hands to acquire perfect equality.

As soon as Ex. 1 is mastered, go on to Ex.2 without stopping on this note.

(3-4) When this exercise is mastered, recommence the preceding one, and play both together four times without interruption; the fingers will gain considerably by practising these exercises, and those following, in this way.

(1) The fourth and fifth fingers being naturally weak, it should be observed that this exercise, and those following it up to Nº 31, are intended to render them as strong and agile as the second and third.

(2-3-4) Before beginning to practise № 3, play through the preceding exercises once or twice without stopping. When № 3 is mastered, practise № 4, and then № 5, and as soon as they are thoroughly learned play through all three at least four times without interruption, not stopping until the last note on page 6. The entire work should be practised in this manner. Therefore, when playing the numbers in the First Part, stop only on the last note on pp. **3, 6, 9, 12, 15, 18,** and **21.**

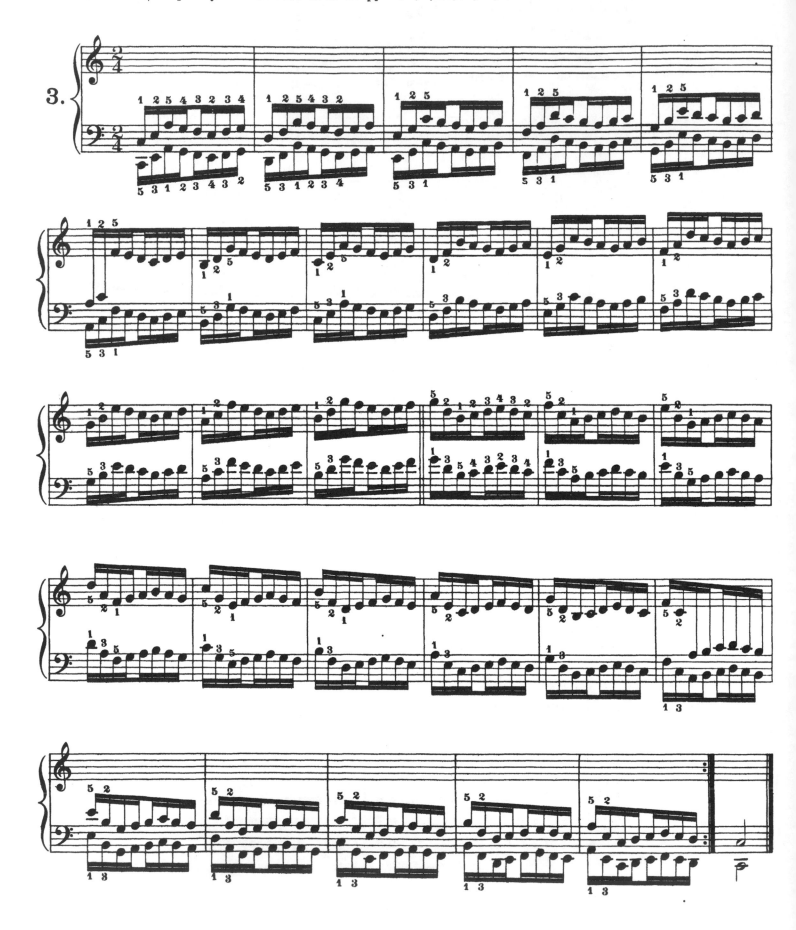

(3-4-5) (1) Special exercise for the 3rd, 4th and 5th fingers of the hand.

(1-2-3-4-5) We repeat, that the fingers should be lifted high, and with precision, until this entire volume is mastered.

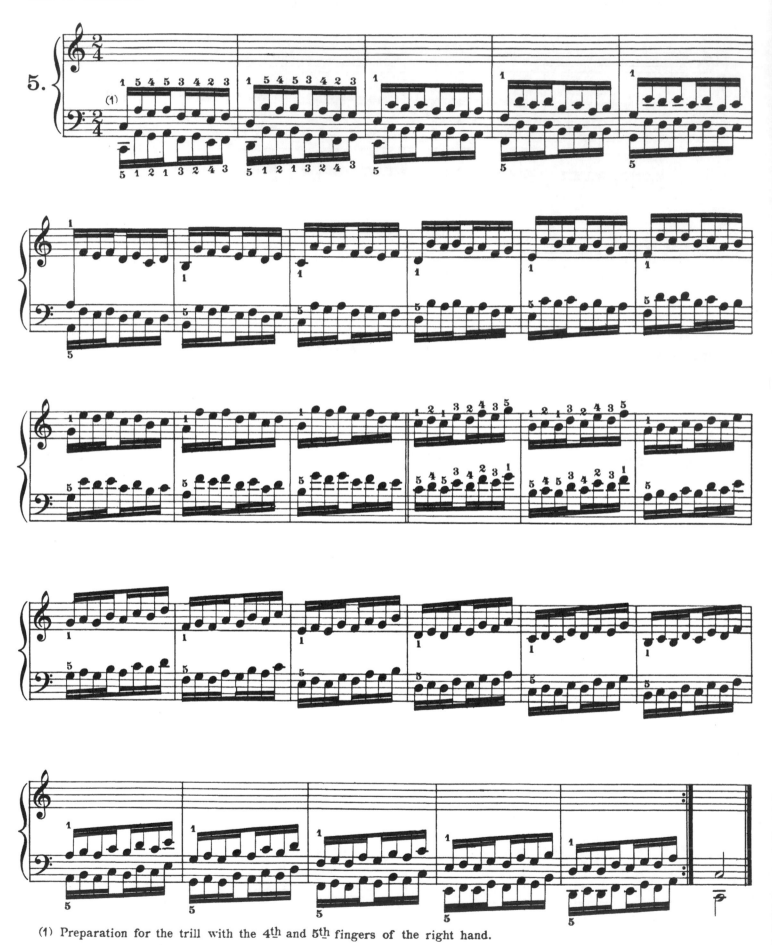

(1) Preparation for the trill with the 4th and 5th fingers of the right hand.

(5) To obtain the good results which we promise those who study this work, it is indispensable to play daily, at least once, the exercises already learned.

(3-4-5) Exercise of the greatest importance for the 3rd, 4th and 5th fingers.

(1-2-3-4-5) Very important exercise for all five fingers.

Extension of the 4th and 5th, and general finger-exercise.

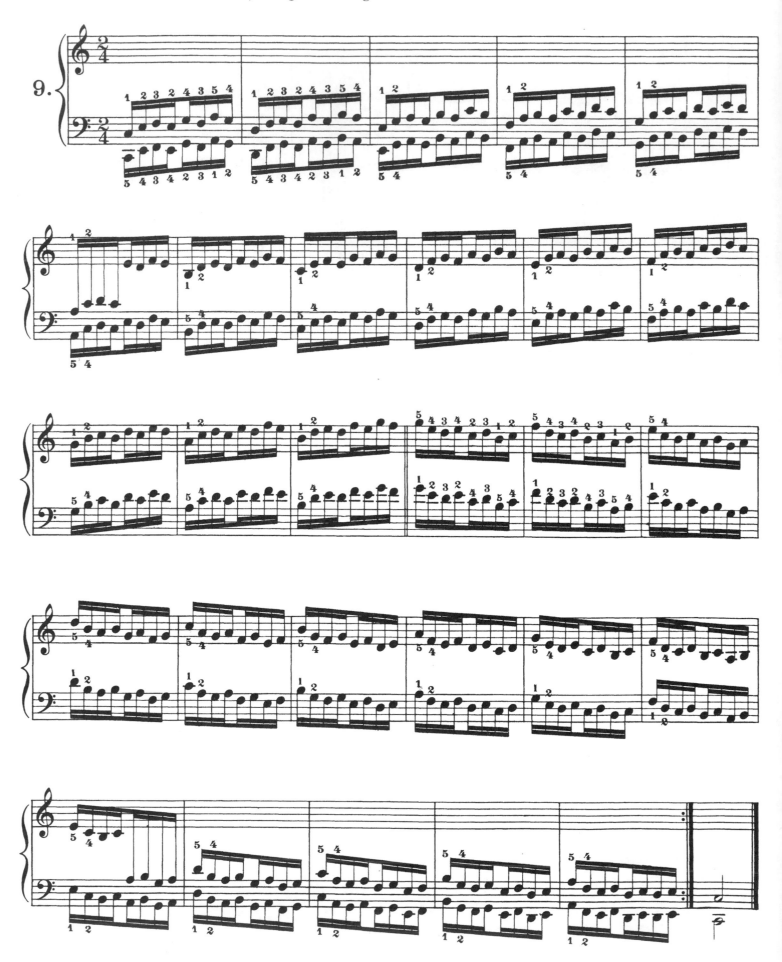

(3-4) Preparation for the trill, for the 3rd and 4th fingers of the left hand in ascending (1); and for the 3rd and 4th of the right, descending (2).

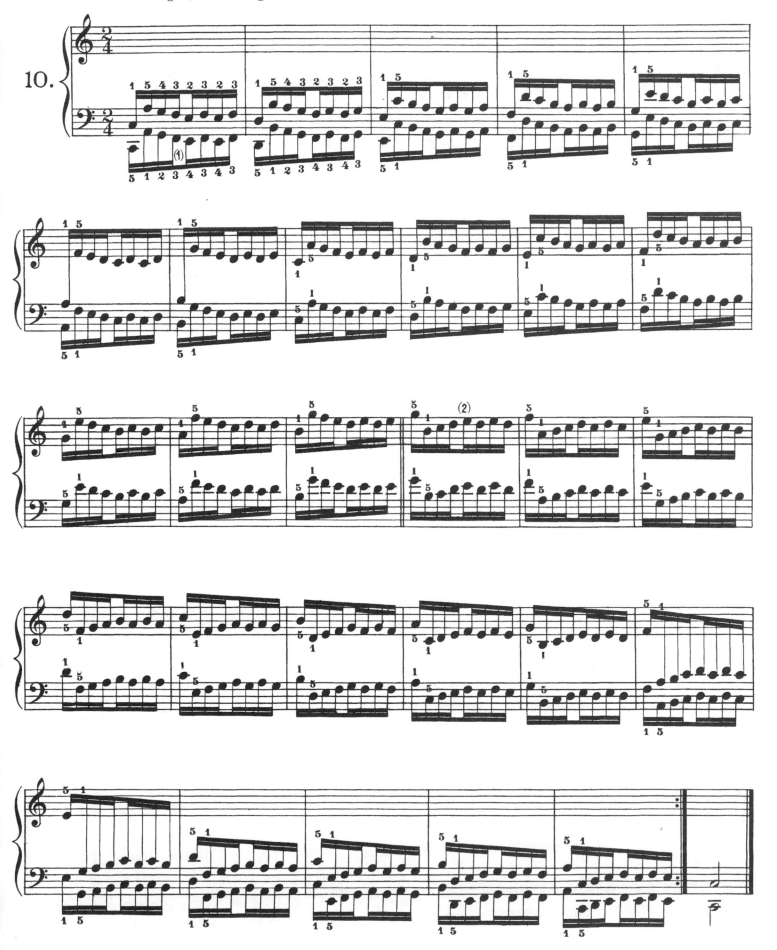

(3-4-5) Another preparation for the trill, for the 4th and 5th fingers.

Extension of 1-5, and exercise for 3-4-5.

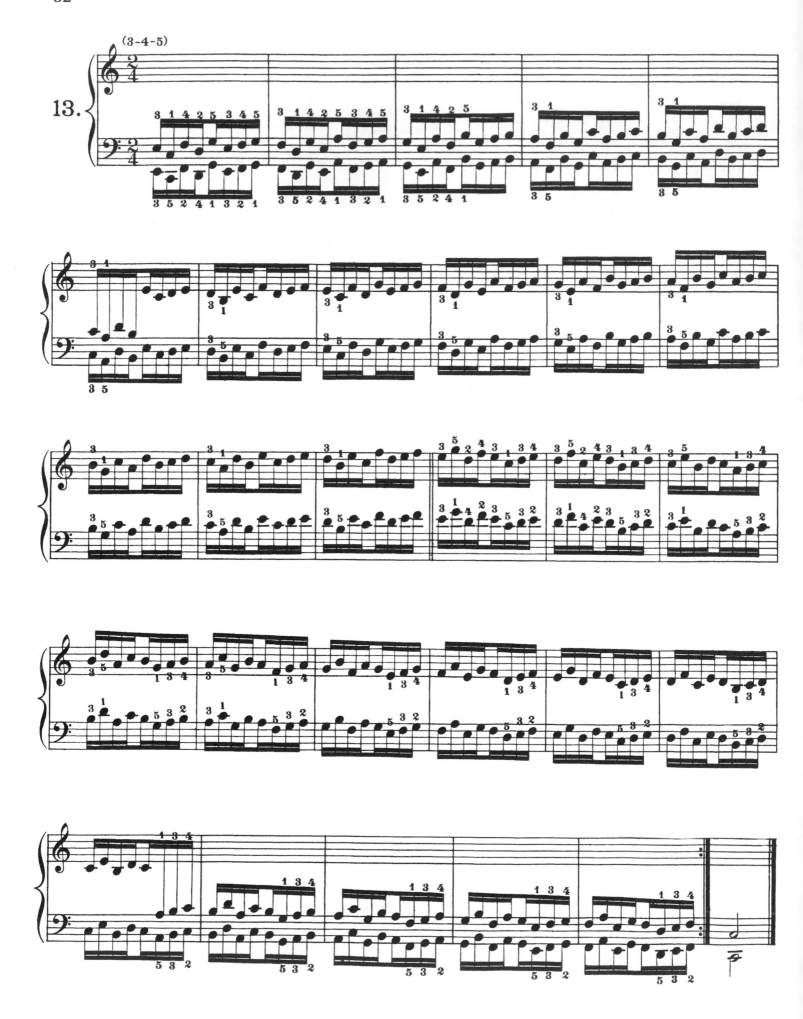

(3-4) Another preparation for the trill, for the 3rd and 4th fingers.

14.

Extension of 1-2, and exercise for all 5 fingers.

Extension of **3-5**, and exercise for **3-4-5**.

Extension of 1-2, 2-4, 4-5, and exercise for 3-4-5.

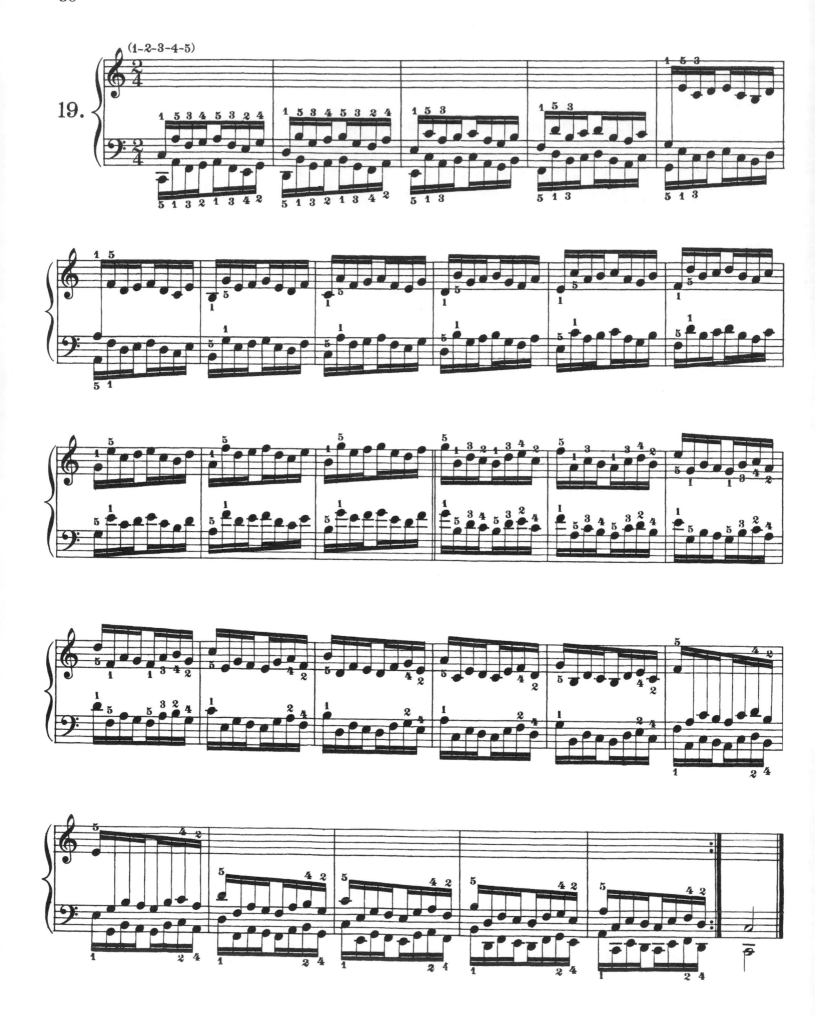

Extension of 2-4, 4-5, and exercise for 2-3-4.

20.

End of Part I.

After having mastered this First Part, play it through once or twice daily for some time before commencing the study of the Second ("transcendent") Part; by so doing, one is sure to obtain every possible advantage that this work promises. Complete mastery of Part I gives the key to the difficulties found in Part II.

TECHNICAL STUDIES
Section I

Louis Plaidy
(1810–1874)

Exercises without moving the Hand
a, Exercises for 2 Fingers
(Slow Trill)

Rules: 1. In addition to the rules given under II. (Rules for the study of Finger-exercises,) the scholar must take care that the unemployed fingers (particularly the 5th.) be neither extended nor contracted, but that they retain the rounded position which has been above described. 2. In these exercises, as well as those following, (N⁰. 12 to N⁰. 81,) the hand is very apt to turn from side to side. The scholar must by no means yield to this tendency. 3. The Trill often tempts one to practice too rapidly. But it cannot be urged too often, that in order to acquire a full and perfect shake it must be practiced *very slowly* with a firm, precise touch and by raising the fingers, (rather high.) (*

*) After having acquired a moderate degree of facility, a more rapid execution may be attempted. The first Exercise, f. i., as follows:

Note: It is perhaps advisable to commence the study of Five-Finger Exercises with Sect. II., in order that the Fingers may be trained to retain their proper position when not occupied.

12. b, Exercises for 3 Fingers.

21. Exercises for 4 Fingers.

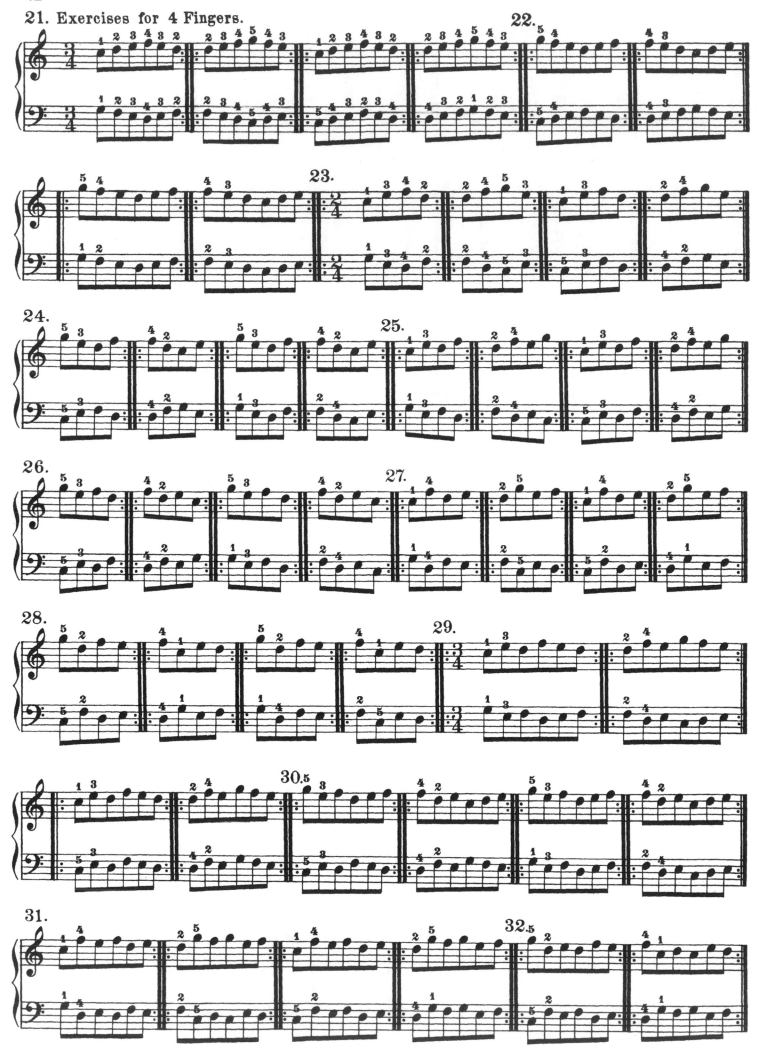

33.

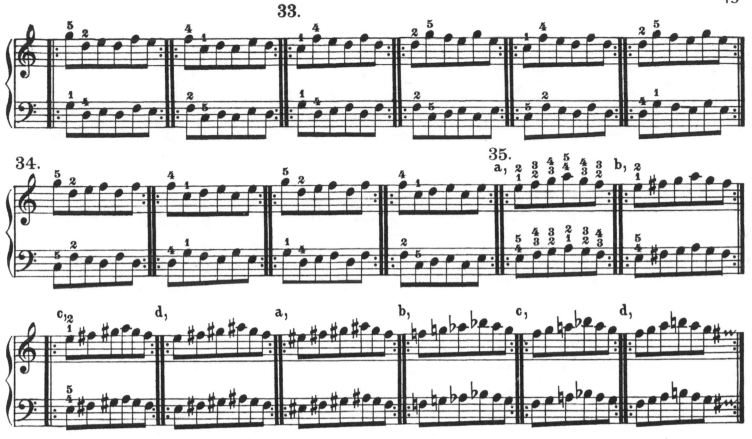

34.

35.

The parallel motion, which is not given in the following examples, is to be supplied by the play-er, by simply duplicating the treble.

36. d, Exercises for 5 Fingers.

37.

38.

39.

40.

41.

42. D flat major.

43. B flat major.

44. B-major.

45. E flat major.

46. C sharp minor.

47. A flat minor.

48. F sharp minor.

49. E minor.

50. F minor.

51. B flat minor.

52. A flat major.

53. D flat minor.

54. G major.

55. F major.

56. C minor.

57. F sharp major.

58. B minor.

59.   60.   61.   62.

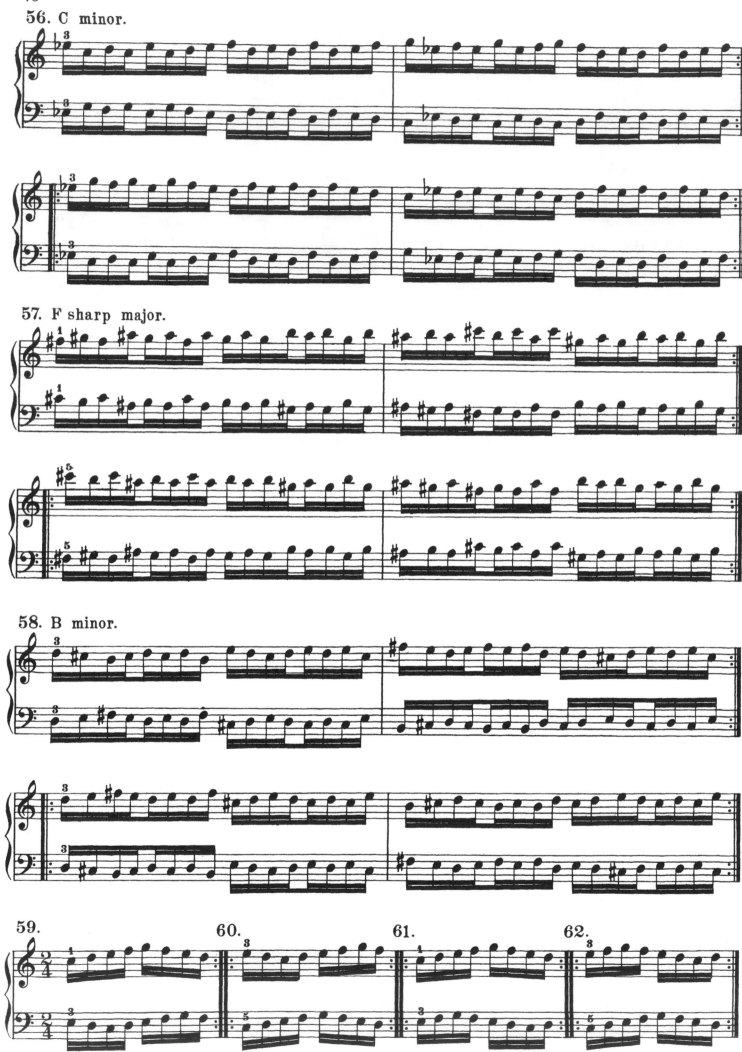

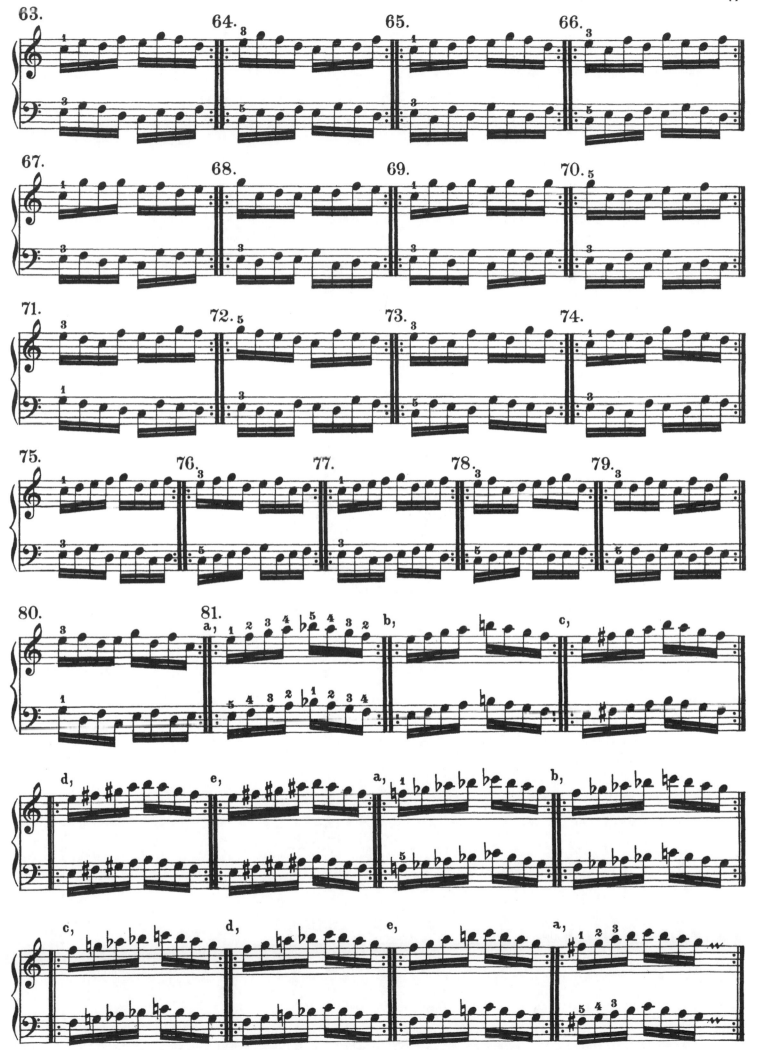

PREPARATORY EXERCISES
Op. 16

Aloys Schmitt
(1788–1866)

for acquiring
the greatest possible independence and
evenness of the fingers

Repeat each Exercise at least ten or twenty times, but omit the closing note until the final repetition. At first, practise each hand separately, then both together, always keeping the hands steady and quiet. Practise each Exercise slowly at first; increase the tempo gradually as the fingers acquire the necessary strength and flexibility.

It is advisable to practise these Exercises in the keys and without changing the fingering.

PIANOFORTE STUDIES

Friedrich Wieck
(1785–1873)

Section I

The first exercises should be played by heart, and transposed into various keys.

*) Play slowly, with the firm "pressure-touch" and not with the ordinary "hammer-stroke."

With the same shading and phrasing as in the preceding.

*) By "Hineinlegen" Fr. Wieck means the firm "pressure-touch."

3.

In ascending succession.

etc.

4.

legato   staccato

In contrary motion.   Ascending.

etc.

5.

Also practise thus:

etc.

SCALES AND CHORDS

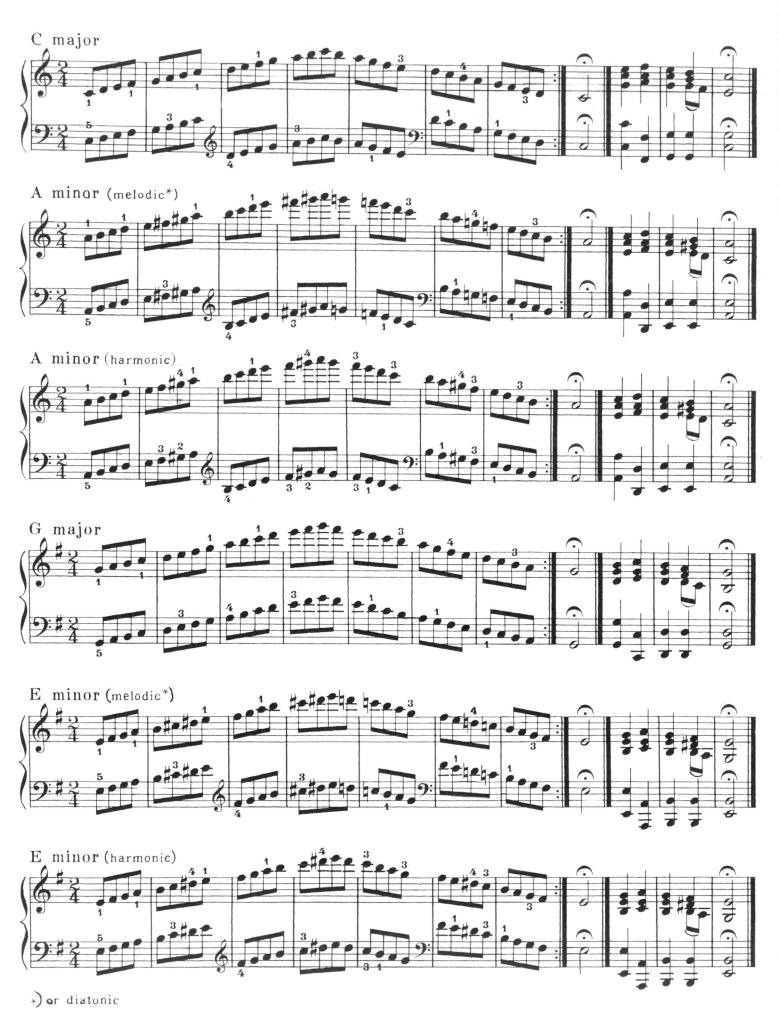

C major

A minor (melodic*)

A minor (harmonic)

G major

E minor (melodic*)

E minor (harmonic)

*) or diatonic

D major

B minor (melodic)

B minor (harmonic)

A major

F-sharp minor (melodic)

F-sharp minor (harmonic)

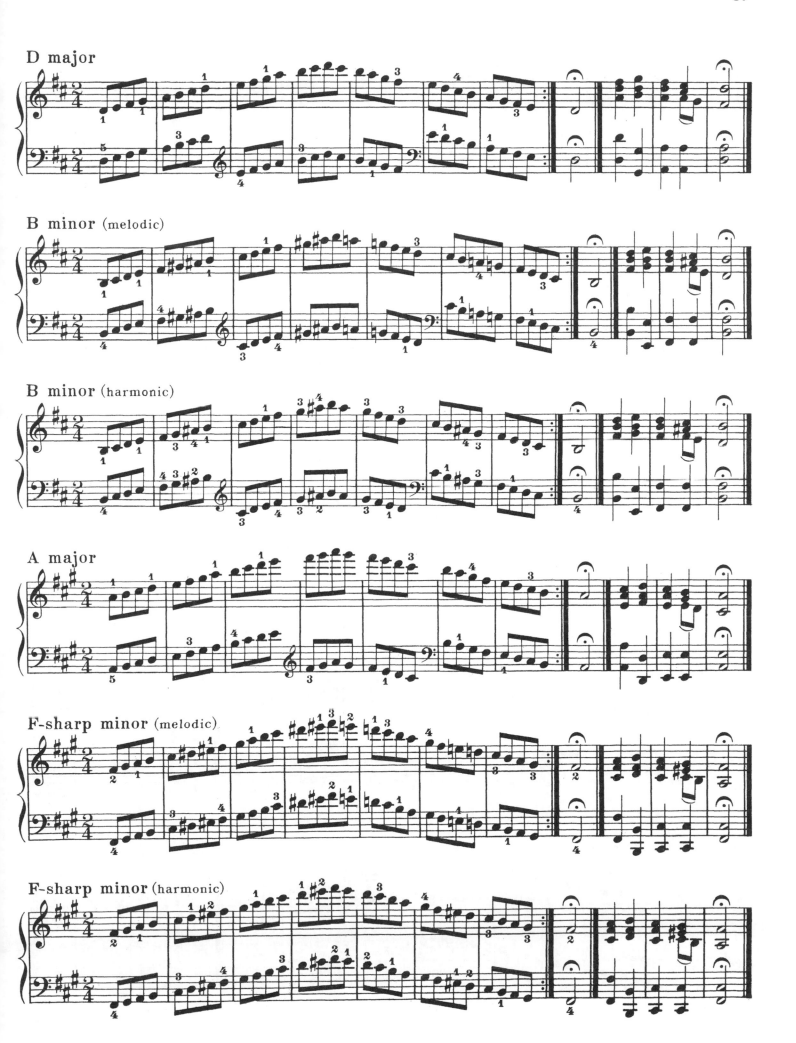

58

E major

C-sharp minor (melodic)

C-sharp minor (harmonic)

B major
identical with C-flat major

G-sharp minor (melodic)
identical with A-flat minor

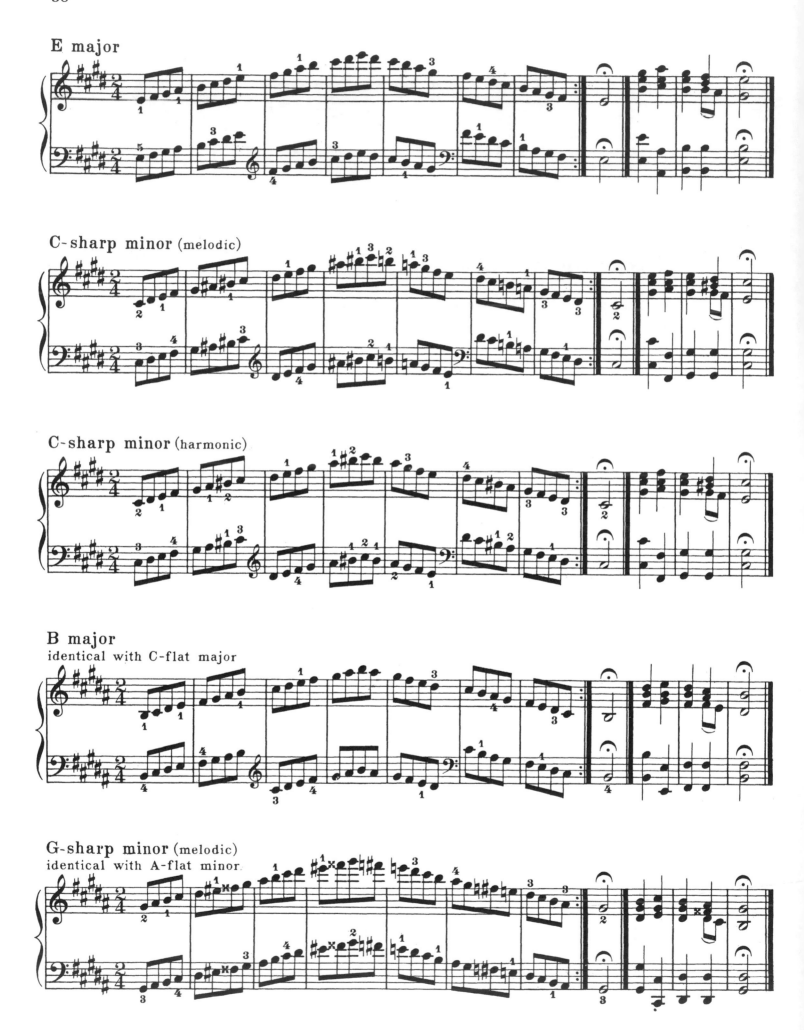

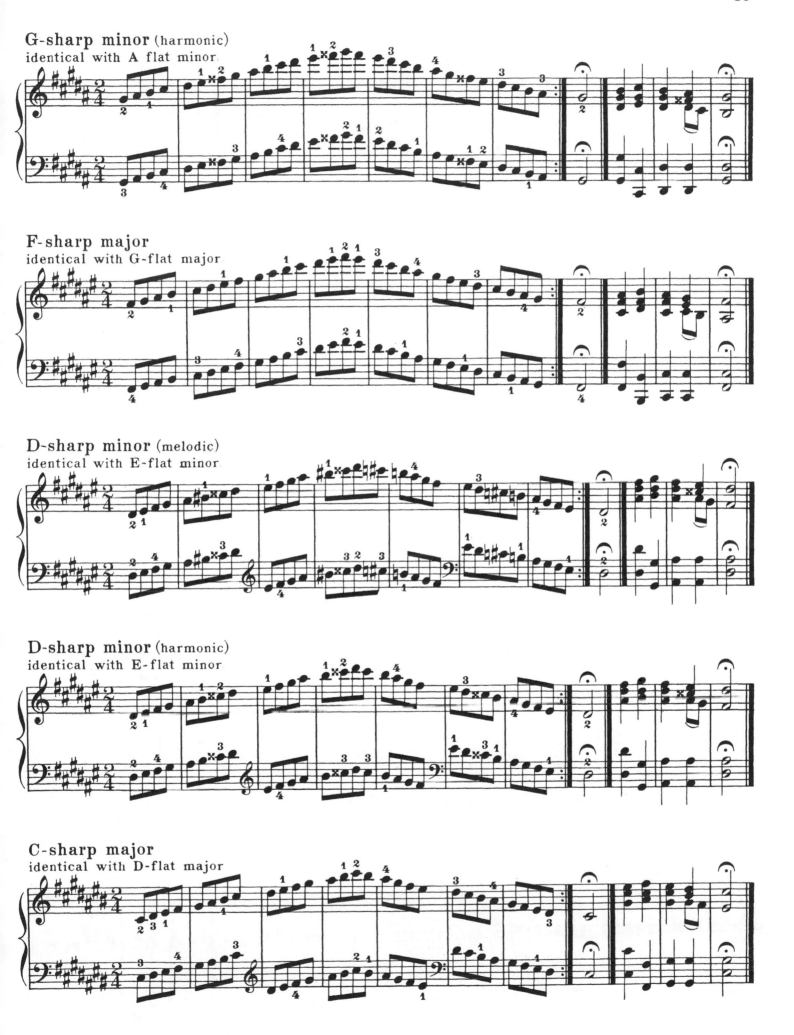

G-sharp minor (harmonic)
identical with A flat minor

F-sharp major
identical with G-flat major

D-sharp minor (melodic)
identical with E-flat minor

D-sharp minor (harmonic)
identical with E-flat minor

C-sharp major
identical with D-flat major

C-flat major
identical with B major

A-flat minor (melodic)
identical with G-sharp minor

A-flat minor (harmonic)
identical with G-sharp minor

G-flat major
identical with F-sharp major

E-flat minor (melodic)
identical with D-sharp minor

E-flat minor (harmonic)
identical with D-sharp minor

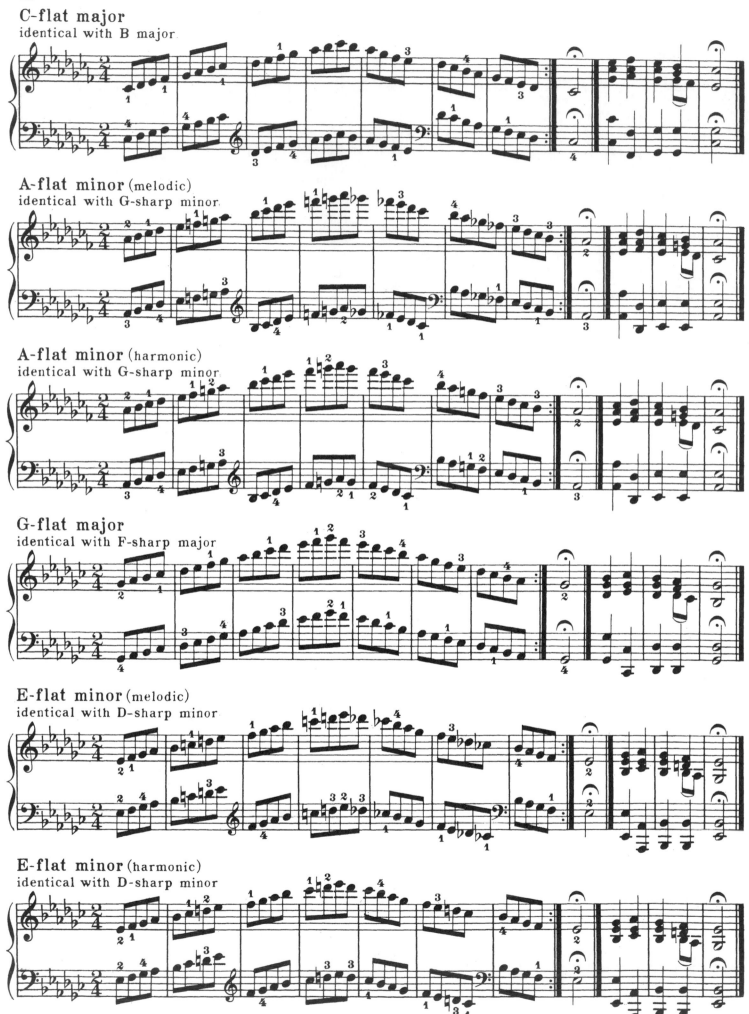

D-flat major
identical with C-sharp major

B-flat minor (melodic)

B-flat minor (harmonic)

A-flat major

F minor (melodic)

F minor (harmonic)

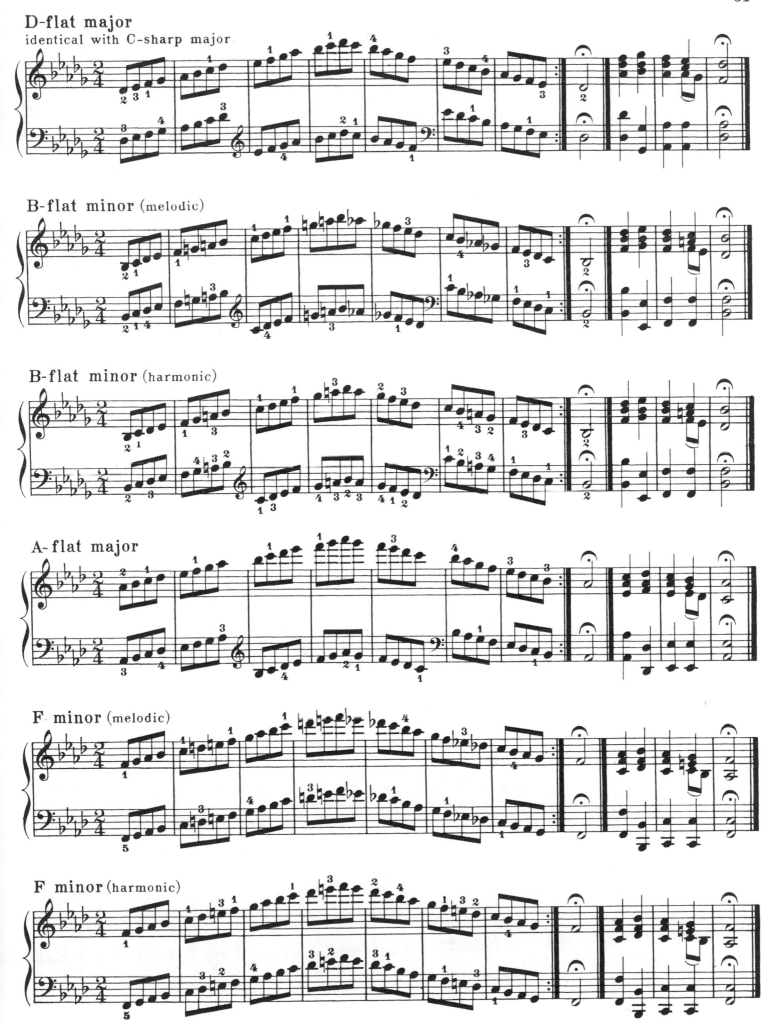

E-flat major.

C minor (melodic).

C minor (harmonic).

B-flat major.

G minor (melodic).

G minor (harmonic).

F major

D minor (melodic)

D minor (harmonic)

The chromatic Scale

*) Scale, combining the Major and Minor

*) Constructed by Moritz Hauptmann and occurs sometimes in modern Music.